Inventors and Creators

Henry
Ford

Inventors and Creators

Henry
Ford

Sheila Wyborny

KIDHAVEN PRESS

THOMSON
✦
GALE

Detroit • New York • San Diego • San Francisco
Boston • New Haven, Conn. • Waterville, Maine
London • Munich

Cover Photo: Henry Ford sitting in his first car.

Library of Congress Cataloging-in-Publication Data

Wyborny, Sheila, 1950–
  Henry Ford / by Sheila Wyborny
    p. cm. — (Inventors and Creators)
  Includes bibliographical references and index.
Summary: Discusses the life of Henry Ford, including his childhood, years as an apprentice, his invention of the automobile, the establishment of the Ford Motor Company and the evolution of the Ford car until 1947.
  ISBN 0-7377-1286-4 (hardback)
    1. Ford, Henry, 1863–1947—Juvenile literature. 2. Industrialists—United States—Biography—Juvenile literature. 3. Automobile industry and trade—United States—Biography—Juvenile literature. 4. Automobile engineers—United States—Biography—Juvenile literature. [1. Ford, Henry, 1863–1947. 2. Industrialists. 3. Automobile industry and trade—Biography.] I. Title. II. Series.
  TL140.F6 W93 2002
  338.7'6292'092—dc21

2001006267

Contents

Chapter One

Down on the Farm

Henry Ford was born on July 30, 1863, on a farm near Dearborn, Michigan. At the age of twenty-one, Ford's father, William, emigrated from Ireland with his parents and his three sisters in the spring of 1847, traveling by ship to the United States. William's mother died on the ship during the voyage and was buried at sea.

Henry's mother, Mary Litogot O'Hern, was orphaned at the age of three and adopted and raised by the O'Hern family. William and Mary met when he worked on the O'Hern farm. Henry was the first child of William and Mary Ford. He was followed by brothers John, William, and Robert, and sisters Margaret and Jane.

A Farming Family

Henry's earliest memory of the family farm was of a pleasant time he shared with his father and one of his brothers.

"The first thing I remember in my life is my father taking my brother John and myself to see a bird's nest under a large oak. . . . John was so young he could not walk. Father carried him. I being two years older could run along with them. . . . I remember the nest with four eggs and also the bird and hearing its song."[1]

Henry led an active life as a farm child. His family taught him how to care for the animals and to recognize the names and habits of wild animals.

From their mother, the Ford children learned responsibility. Farm chores came before fun. "You must earn the right to play,"[2] she told her children. His mother supported Henry in all that he did. She especially supported his unique personality. She told him that being different showed strength of character.

Mary Ford encouraged learning by teaching each of her children to read before they started school. Henry began his formal education in 1870. He attended the Scotch Settlement School, a one-room schoolhouse. It was the same school his mother had attended as a child.

Henry was bright and curious, but he was not a top student. He would daydream and sometimes get into trouble with his best friend, Edsel Ruddiman. Henry and Edsel invented their own alphabet so that the teacher would not understand what they had written if she caught them passing

Henry Ford at three years of age.

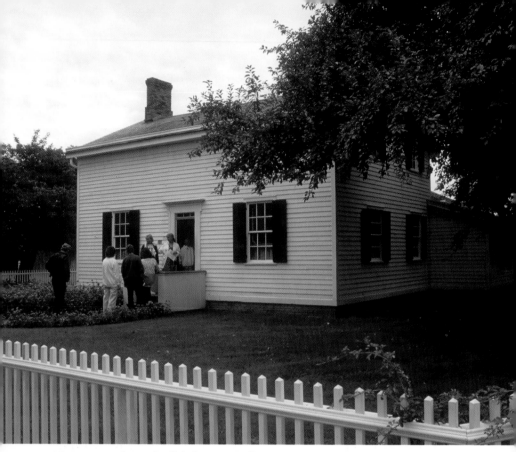
Henry was born in this house in Dearborn, Michigan, in 1863.

notes in class. Henry and Edsel received many after-school lectures from their teacher.

Henry the Tinkerer

Although Henry and his brothers and sisters played together, from an early age Henry was different from his siblings. While his brothers liked to play ball, Henry spent time on his own, tinkering with different items to see what made them work. While his brothers and sisters did farm chores, Henry took apart machines and tools and examined the parts. Everyone in the family knew that Henry liked to tinker. In fact, when any of the children were given wind-up toys, they had to keep them away from Henry because he would take them apart, but he could not always put them back together properly.

Henry's father wanted him to be a farmer. Henry, as eldest son, was expected to learn how to run the farm. But instead of doing farm chores, he preferred to work with the tools in the machine shop.

Henry's tinkering sometimes caused trouble. Once he asked his father what would happen if he plugged the spout of a boiling kettle. Because his father's answer did not tell him all he wanted to know, Henry plugged the spout of the kettle. The kettle exploded, spraying scalding water all over the kitchen. A sharp, jagged piece of the kettle cut a gash in Henry's face. Such accidents did not put a stop to Henry's curiosity. He decided he would try to build a real steam engine. When he was satisfied that his engine would work, he set it up by the school fence. The metal Henry used to make the boiler that produced the steam was not strong enough to withstand the pressure of the steam. Once again, Henry's experimentation caused an explosion. This time the damage was more serious. Both Henry and another student were injured and part of the school fence was destroyed. Henry's father had to rebuild the fence.

Henry Loses His Mother

When Henry was twelve, his mother died shortly after childbirth. Henry became more withdrawn from the rest of his family, tinkering with gadgets into the night.

Henry's mother, Mary, died when Henry was twelve years old.

Without his mother, Henry felt lost and lonely. He spoke very little. His father was concerned about his son. For Henry's thirteenth birthday, his father gave him a watch. He knew Henry would not be satisfied until he understood how the tiny wheels and springs worked, and he hoped that the watch would provide his son with something to occupy his time instead of dwelling on his mother's death.

Henry did not have tools tiny enough to work on the watch, so he made tools from his mother's old darning needles and other items from her sewing box. Soon he could take the watch apart and put it back together like an expert, but still his mother was never far from his thoughts.

He spoke of her in later years. "[She was] of that rarest type, one who so loved her children that she did not care whether they loved her. What I mean by this is that she would do whatever she considered necessary for our welfare, even if she thereby lost our good will."[3]

Henry felt very lost and lonely after his mother died.

Henry was going through a sad time in his life, but something was about to happen that would point him toward his destiny.

A Born Engineer

One day, Henry's father took him on a trip to Detroit, Michigan, in the family's horse-drawn wagon. As they traveled along, they saw a strange machine chugging slowly down the road toward them. As they drew closer, they could see that it was a farm machine called a thresher. Henry was particularly interested in the thresher's engine. Henry had seen engines before, but this was different. All of the engines he had seen were moved from place to place by horses and were used to run sawmills and farming

Henry was fascinated when he saw a farm machine like this one moving under its own power with its own engine.

machines. This time, the engine caused this unusual machine to move under its own power. He jumped from the wagon and ran to the man who operated the machine.

Henry was full of questions and the man, an engineer, patiently answered all of them. It was this event that convinced Henry he wanted to be an engineer.

Although Henry remained on the farm for several more years to help his father, William Ford finally understood that his son would never be happy as a farmer. He took Henry back to Detroit, a distance of eight miles from the family farm in Dearborn, Michigan, and found him a job as an apprentice at the Flower Machine Shop. Henry learned to design and make iron parts for machines. At the age of seventeen, Henry Ford was on his own, and on his way toward realizing his dreams.

Chapter Two

Ford Follows His Dream

For the first time in his young life, Henry Ford was away from home. Moving from the farm to the city was a great change. It was an exciting time and also a difficult one.

Learning His Craft

Ford learned that being an apprentice was hard work. He had to learn every step in making the products for the Flower Machine Shop, from drawing plans, to molding, to polishing the final product. He also learned that an apprentice's wages, $2.50 a week, would not support him.

To earn extra money, Ford took an evening job at a jewelry store repairing watches. All the time he had spent tinkering with watches and clocks back at the family farm gave him the skills he needed for this job. He worked in a back room, out of the sight of the customers. His employer felt that if the customers saw how young the repairman was, they would not want him working on their timepieces.

Ford, seen here at age twenty-five, became an apprentice after moving from his farm to the city.

A little less than a year later, Ford felt he had learned all he could from the machine shop and was ready to learn new skills. He became an apprentice at the Detroit Drydock Company, a shipbuilding company. His first training was in the engine shop, where he saw the problems of using steam engines. They used large amounts of fuel, coal, or wood to heat the boilers. The ships had to carry their fuel, which added to the weight of the load. The company knew it needed to solve this problem and was working on an experimental engine. This was the first time Ford saw an internal combustion engine. The engine was more efficient and powerful than a steam engine. This new engine made a great impression on young Ford, and he would put the valuable information he learned to practical use in future years.

But soon this apprenticeship also came to an end, and it was time for Ford to return to Dearborn and put his new mechanical skills to work.

A Home of His Own

In 1882 with his apprenticeships completed, nineteen-year-old Ford was hired as a certified machinist for the Westinghouse Company. He traveled around Michigan for several years, setting up and operating steam engines for farmers. In the winter months when farmers had no need of his services, he set up a machine shop on his father's farm, where he spent the off-season designing and building a lightweight engine.

He later spoke of the engines he operated as a young man in his twenties and of his plans for the future. "They could make twelve miles an hour on the road. . . . Even before that time I had the idea of making some kind of light steam car that would take the place of horses."[4]

But Ford did not spend all of his time working. He enjoyed parties and was quite a good dancer. While at a dance in 1885, he met pretty, dark-eyed Clara Bryant.

Mrs. Clara Bryant Ford was interested in her husband's ideas.

She was a good dancer, too. Not only did they share several dances that night, but she was truly interested in hearing his ideas about engines. Meeting Clara started Ford thinking about a home and a family of his own.

Ford was in a good position to start a family. His father had given him a parcel of land, and Henry had built a lumber mill on it. He then sold fine hardwoods from his land and repaired machinery from neighboring farms. Ford began courting Clara and when he felt that he had saved enough money to support a family, he and Clara were married in Dearborn on April 11, 1888.

Although working hard to support his wife and himself, Ford did not lose sight of his dream: creating a lightweight steam engine. In 1891 he saw a gasoline-powered internal combustion engine operate at a bottling plant in Detroit. He became inspired by the many kinds of functions that could be done with such a machine.

But Ford needed more experience to build a practical internal combustion engine, so he and his wife moved to Detroit. Ford went to work for the Edison Illuminating Company.

Crazy Henry

In 1893 Ford built his first gasoline-powered engine. It was crudely made, but it worked. This was also the year of the birth of Henry and Clara Ford's only child, a son they named Edsel in honor of Ford's old school friend.

Clara kept busy taking care of the new baby. She also helped her husband in his experiments. Ford's internal combustion engine was first started in the family kitchen, over the sink, with Clara carefully dripping gasoline into the engine from an oilcan. Following the success of this engine, Ford worked to create a larger

Ford built his first gasoline-powered engine in this shed.

model. He did most of his work in the shed outside the house to avoid jeopardizing the health and safety of his wife and baby. Many nights, neighbors heard pounding, grinding, and sputtering from the shed. "Crazy Henry," as he was called by neighbors and coworkers, would sometimes work far into the night. But finally, early on a June morning in 1896, Ford tore the side from the shed and drove forth in his first horseless carriage, which he

19

called the quadricycle. For a horn, Ford had attached a doorbell to the vehicle. The quadricycle made horrible noise and puffed black smoke. Horses reared, dogs barked, and pedestrians leaped for the wooden sidewalks as the strange-looking contraption whizzed past at speeds up to an unbelievable twenty miles per hour.

Soon after completing his first quadricycle, Ford drove it to the family farm, a distance of about ten miles, and took his family for rides. His sister, Margaret,

Ford sits in his quadricycle.

recalled "the great speed and sense of bewilderment"[5] she felt during her ride.

Encouragement, Trial, and Error

The same year he created the quadricycle, Ford's supervisor, Alexander Dow, took him to the convention of the Association of Edison Illuminating Companies in New York. Here, he introduced Ford to fellow inventor Thomas Edison. Dow told Edison about Ford's automobile with the internal combustion engine. Edison was impressed and offered him encouragement. "Young man, that's the thing; you have it. Keep right at it."[6] Edison's words made a deep impression on Ford.

The quadricycle was a beginning, but Ford wanted to create a practical automobile. Although other automobiles had been developed, Ford wanted to produce one that would be better and faster than the others. With this in mind, he began working on a new design.

By 1899 Ford had left his job with the Edison Illuminating Company and was working full time on his new car. By the end of that year, he had completed the new model and had the financial backing of a wealthy lumberman. Together, they formed the Detroit Automobile Company. However, the automobile Ford designed did not get the attention of buyers. When Ford wanted to make changes to improve the car's design, the lumberman and the other backers did not support him, and the company soon went out of business.

But Ford stuck to his ideas and soon had another plan. Because automobile racing was a popular sport,

Ford decided to build a race car. On October 10, 1901, Ford's 26-horsepower racing car beat that of the well-known racing driver Alexander Winton. The publicity from this race drew the attention of more wealthy people. They financed a second automobile company,

Fellow inventor Thomas Edison encouraged Ford to continue working on his ideas for the automobile.

Ford stands beside his 999 race car. Car racer Barney Oldfield is seated in the vehicle.

the Henry Ford Company, but that company also failed after just a few months.

Still, Ford continued to work on his designs and with Tom Cooper built two 80-horsepower racers, the Arrow and the 999. Tom Cooper was a bicycle racer who had become a car racer. The 999, driven by another bicycle racer, Barney Oldfield, won the Challenger's Cup at Grosse Pointe, Michigan, in 1902. By this time, Ford had yet another financial backer, Alexander Malcomson, a Detroit coal merchant. With this partnership, Ford had a third opportunity to produce his automobiles for the public.

Chapter Three

A Dynasty Is Born

Because he had left his job to work full time on designing his car, Ford and Clara were often short of money. Times were so hard that they had to move in with Ford's father. William Ford worried that his son might never be successful. Nevertheless, Henry Ford's determination did not waiver. His partnership with Malcomson would soon be hugely successful. It began a new era in the automobile industry: the manufacture of practical automobiles for average people.

Growing Pains

On June 15, 1903, the Ford Motor Company was formed. Ford set up shop in an old icehouse on Mack Avenue in Detroit, Michigan. Ford hired ten workers at wages of $1.50 a day to assemble the automobiles at Mack Avenue, but the frames and parts would be made elsewhere. The Dodge brothers, John and Harold, were contracted to build the framework for the cars, and parts were made by other contractors. The materials were all brought to the Mack Avenue shop and assembled there.

The Ford Motor Company began in an old icehouse on Mack Avenue in Detroit, Michigan.

This method of building cars disturbed Ford because he did not have control over how the parts and frames were made. He worried that the workers in these other plants might not be supervised as carefully in the making of the parts as his workers were supervised in the assembly of the automobiles. Ford's worries about quality control were soon justified.

By July, the first Model A rolled out of the Mack Avenue factory, but soon the Ford Motor Company received complaints. The cars overheated and dripped oil. They could not climb inclines. Ford took responsibility for these problems. "When one of my cars breaks down, I know I am to blame,"[7] he said.

Despite complaints and problems, Ford's first automobile made the Ford Motor Company the leading car manufacturer of its day. Ford became known as a man who took responsibility for his cars' problems and took action to solve the problems. With Ford's reputation behind it, the company grew. But even as the first Model A made a name for the Ford Motor Company, Ford had plans for a future car, one that would be lighter, stronger, and easier to repair.

The Tin Lizzie

The Model T Ford, known as the "Tin Lizzie," was first produced in 1908. It was well made, affordable, and most repairs could easily be done by the owner. It was also well suited to all kinds of road conditions. Each Tin Lizzie produced was identical to the one before it.

Ford believed that the best way to build an automobile was to develop a good, serviceable model and then to make all of the cars alike, even the color. "A customer can have a car in any color he wants so long as it is black,"[8] he joked.

Ford also believed that making all of his automobiles alike was good business. More cars could be produced in a shorter time, which helped lower the cost of each car. By lowering the cost of the cars, more people could afford to buy them and so more cars would be sold,

The Model T Ford is also known as the "Tin Lizzie."

making more money for the company. Sales figures over the years proved him right. A Ford automobile had cost $950 in 1905, but by 1913 the Ford Motor Company had been able to lower the price of each car to $490. Tin Lizzie, the Model T, became the best-selling automobile in America.

By this time, Ford and his partner, Alexander Malcomson, had parted company. Malcomson had wanted Ford to produce expensive luxury cars for the rich, but Ford continued producing affordable automobiles for the general public. Malcomson left to

A Ford sales office offers Model T cars for sale. The Model T was the best-selling car in America by 1913.

form his own automobile company. But even without Malcomson, the company continued to grow rapidly.

The Ford Motor Company, which quickly outgrew its Mack Avenue plant and also became too large for its later plant on Piquette Avenue, needed more space. Ford also wanted to take mass production a step further, and so he put plans in motion to build a new automobile plant.

Highland Park

For his new plant, Ford chose a sixty-acre racetrack in Highland Park, just northwest of Detroit. Although the company moved to the new site in 1910, it was not completely built until 1914.

He wanted a plant where every single step in the creation of an automobile could be made on site. At the Highland Park plant, Ford had complete control. There were even on-site furnaces where metals were cast into automobile parts and upholstery shops where the seats were made. In its first year of production, before the plant was completely built, the Highland Park plant put nineteen thousand Model Ts on the roads. By the time the plant was totally completed, it was producing nearly eighty thousand automobiles a year.

In its first year of production, the Highland Park plant built nineteen thousand Model T cars.

Chiefly responsible for the rapid production rate were the use of assembly lines and conveyor belts. In an assembly line, each worker does one specific job in the building of the car. For instance, one worker might put on all of the right-hand doors and another worker would put on all of the left-hand doors. Instead of workers having to walk to parts, pick them up, and bring them back to put on the automobile, conveyor belts brought the parts to the workers. The conveyor belts were about waist high, so the workers did not even have to bend over

Assembly lines made it possible to produce Ford cars quickly.

to pick up the parts. These factors greatly cut down the time it took to produce one automobile.

Highland Park Workers

While these changes in production resulted in mass production of less-expensive cars, workers in the Highland Park plant were not happy. Performing one task over and over, day after day, was stressful and exhausting. Also, an average worker's wages would not support his family, which made for low morale in the workplace. The workers complained and Ford listened.

In 1914 workers' wages were raised from $2.50 to $5.00 a day. Word of the raise spread. The newspapers praised Ford. The workers were happy with their raises, but Ford's doubling his workers' wages caused problems. Many people were out of work at this time and began mobbing the plant, asking for jobs. They even came to Ford's home in such great numbers that the Fords were forced to move. Also, other automobile manufacturers were angry with Ford because he paid his workers so much more than they paid their own employees. But despite the problems, production of Ford automobiles continued to rise. Wages were high. But Ford did not remain popular for the rest of his career. Some of his choices brought success, while other choices created conflict.

Chapter Four

Success, Conflict, and the End of an Era

F ord felt that his company should keep using the same designs for his cars, and for a number of years his plans worked with spectacular results in sales and profits. For a while, everyone associated with Ford automobiles, from assembly line workers to board members, were happy. But when the time came for Ford to change his automobile and his strategies, he was not willing to do so. He thought that an idea or a product, once successful, should always be successful. Finally the time came when even the strong-willed Ford had to accept that times were changing.

The New Model A

By the mid 1920s the Tin Lizzie, once praised for its practicality, was considered old fashioned. The young adults of the Roaring Twenties wanted luxury and glamour. They wanted something different. But Tin Lizzie looked the same, rattled along the roads the same as it had for nearly twenty years, and it was the same

Strong-willed Ford had to finally accept that times were changing and that he needed to change his automobile design.

color: black. When people laughed and made jokes about the Tin Lizzie, Ford realized he had to make changes in his automobiles if people were to keep buying them.

On May 26, 1927, Ford and his son, Edsel, who had joined the company, followed along the assembly line as

Edsel Ford, Henry Ford's son.

the final Model T was produced. The two men then climbed into the car, drove it to Dearborn, and parked it next to the famous quadricycle. This marked the end of the Model T, but soon a new Ford would rule the roads.

The Highland Park plant closed over the summer. All of the manufacturing equipment had to be rebuilt to produce the new model. On December 1, ads appeared in newspapers across the country. Ford would soon unveil a new car. Crowds gathered at showrooms in the United States and in Europe. Police were called in to control unruly mobs. In London, extra trains were run into the city because so many people wanted to see Ford's new automobile.

That car was the new Model A. With seventeen variations in body style and a choice of four colors, it was a huge success. Also adding to its success was the price range: $495 to $570. Near the price of the old Model T, the new Model A was much less expensive than competitors' cars of the day.

Positive comments poured into the Ford offices. One was a telegram from Hollywood actor Douglas Fairbanks, who said of his wife, actress Mary Pickford, "Mary uses [the] new Ford in preference to all her other cars."[9]

The new Model A was more affordable to buyers than ever. To go with the new model, the Ford Motor Company began financing its automobiles on installment plans. It was now even easier for average people to own automobiles. Monthly payments could be made as the new owner enjoyed the use of the car.

With the new model and the installment payment plan, Henry Ford was once again the leader of the automobile industry. But dark days loomed ahead and

The new Model A was a huge success.

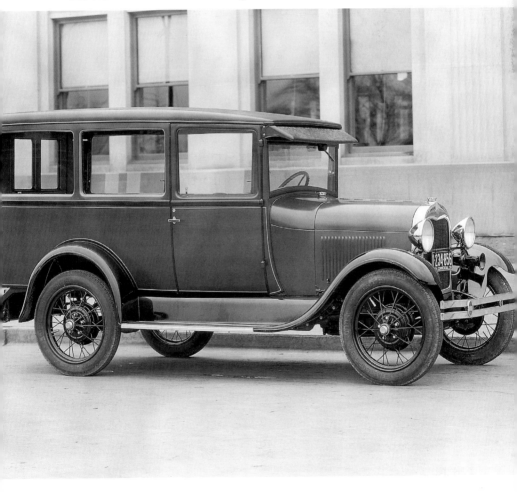

would bring conflict to Ford and his company. It would require all of the creativity and business expertise the man and his organization could muster.

The Great Depression

Tuesday, October 29, 1929, is known as Black Tuesday, or the crash of 1929. On that day, the prices of many stock shares plummeted. Many companies went out of business, many banks failed, and many people were left penniless. Families lost their homes. The country entered a time called the Great Depression.

During the early days of the depression, the Ford Motor Company suffered no ill effects because Henry Ford owned his company outright. He had no shares on the stock exchange. But by 1930 even the Ford Motor Company suffered because people could not afford to buy cars. During 1930 and 1931 the company showed a fall in profits of $40 million and workers' pay, once among the highest wages in the country, was cut.

But even in those dark days, Ford had a plan: the new V8 engine. Before the V8, automobiles had only four cylinders. The more powerful V8 was an eight-cylinder engine. In addition to increasing the speed of the automobile, it also gave a smooth ride. This new Ford automobile sold for as little as $460. Even at the height of the depression, people packed the showrooms for a look at the new Ford automobile with its revolutionary engine.

By 1934, because of the Ford V8, the Ford Motor Company once again showed profits. But Ford's problems were not over.

Even during the dark days of the depression, Ford had a plan, a design for a new V8 engine.

Edsel (left) and Henry Ford display their new V8 engine in 1937.

Bringing the Ford Motor Company back up to a healthy profit margin fell on the workers. Although their wages had been cut when the company suffered huge losses, when the V8 went into production the workers were under pressure to produce more cars and to produce them faster. The days of concern for the workers' welfare were gone. Lunch breaks were cut to fifteen minutes. Working conditions continued to suffer until employees began to push to join the United Auto Workers union. Ford initially resisted, but with his wife's urging, Ford signed a union contract. Under the terms of the contract, the workers decided how fast to run the assembly lines and produce cars, and they also had a say in determining fair wages for themselves.

Although conditions at the Ford Motor Company improved for the workers, the Ford family would soon suffer tragedy.

Ford employees pushed to join the United Auto Workers union and Ford agreed.

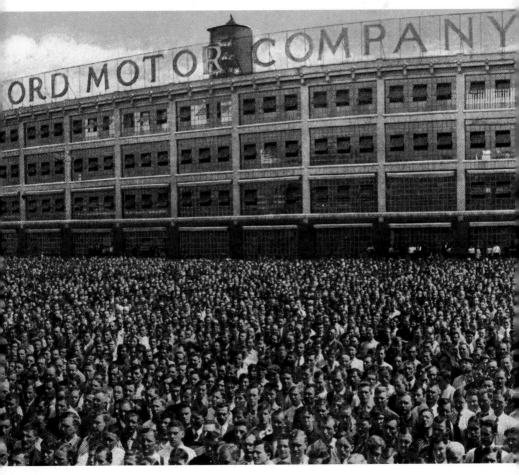

Sad Endings and New Beginnings

The conflict and stress took a toll on Edsel Ford's health. He developed ulcers. But despite his weakened condition, he continued to try to be a positive influence on his father and the company. When Edsel's health continued to fail, more tests were run. He was diagnosed with stomach cancer. Edsel Ford, the only child of Henry and Clara Ford, died in May 1943. He was fifty years old. Henry and Clara's grief was so great that for many weeks following Edsel's death, the Fords could not talk about their son.

At the age of eighty and with a weak heart, Ford once again took over the presidency of the Ford Motor Company. But Ford's family realized that he was in no condition to handle such responsibility. The family persuaded him to hand over the position to his grandson, Henry Ford II, who by then was in his late twenties. With careful planning and hard work, young Henry Ford reorganized the company and restored some of its earlier morale.

He reorganized bookkeeping, an outdated system that was still paying employees in cash, and brought in management experts to restructure and streamline the company. Finally, the elder Henry Ford admitted respect for the leadership qualities he saw in his grandson.

On April 17, 1947, Henry and Clara Ford went to a restaurant for dinner. When they returned home, they decided to go to bed early. As Clara prepared for bed, Ford began a coughing spell. A short time later, eighty-four-year-old Henry Ford was dead.

Henry Ford II, Henry Ford's grandson, became president of the Ford Motor Company in 1945.

More than two hundred thousand people filed by to pay respect as Ford's casket lay in state. On the following Thursday, the day of his funeral, Detroit, known as the city built by the automobile, closed all of its businesses.

Mourners file past Henry Ford's casket.

Henry Ford created a giant industry. His beliefs angered some people and his generosity helped others. But regardless of how his character is judged, the inventor and businessperson did exactly what he said he would do: Henry Ford put the automobile within reach of average, working-class people.

Notes

Chapter 1: Down on the Farm

1. Quoted in Peter Collier and David Horowitz, *The Fords: An American Epic*. New York: Summit Books, 1987, p. 19.
2. Quoted in Collier and Horowitz, *The Fords*, p. 20.
3. Quoted in Collier and Horowitz, *The Fords*, p. 20.

Chapter 2: Ford Follows His Dream

4. Henry Ford, *My Life and Work*. Salem, NH: Ayer Company, 1922, p. 25.
5. Quoted in Collier and Horowitz, *The Fords*, p. 11.
6. Quoted in Carol Gelderman, *Henry Ford: The Wayward Capitalist*. New York: St. Martin's Press, 1981, p. 67.

Chapter 3: A Dynasty Is Born

7. Ford, *My Life and Work*, p. 67.
8. Quoted in Collier and Horowitz, *The Fords*, p. 68.

Chapter 4: Success, Conflict, and the End of an Era

9. Quoted in Gelderman, *Henry Ford*, p. 262.

For Further Exploration

Jacqueline L. Harris, *Henry Ford*. New York: Franklin Watts, 1984. A detailed middle-grade biography with illustrations.

Zachary Kent, *The Story of Henry Ford and the Automobile*. Chicago: Childrens Press, 1990. A brief but well-illustrated biography of Ford.

Hayden Middleton, *Henry Ford*. Oxford, NY: Oxford University Press, 1997. Fairly easy reading for elementary grades.

Barbara Mitchell, *We'll Race You, Henry!* Minneapolis: Carolrhoda Books, 1986. A well-illustrated history of Ford and his automobile.

Robert Quackenbush, *Along Came the Model T! Henry Ford Put the World on Wheels*. New York: Parent's Magazine Press, 1978. Well illustrated and fairly easy reading.

Index

Picture Credits

Cover Photo: © Bettmann/CORBIS

© Bettmann/CORBIS, 10, 15, 27, 28, 35, 42

© Brown Brothers, 17, 23

Culver Pictures, 30, 34

© Hulton/Archive by Getty Images, 7, 11, 20, 25, 41

© Hulton-Deutsch Collection/CORBIS, 12, 37

© Wolfgang Kaehler/CORBIS, 8

© Lake County Museum/CORBIS, 29, 39

Library of Congress, 19

© Stock Montage, Inc., 22

© Underwood & Underwood/CORBIS, 33, 38

About the Author

Sheila Wyborny lives in Houston, Texas, with her husband, Wendell. They like to spend their free time flying their Cessna aircraft and looking for antiques to add to their small collection.